T0197570

The Zoo of Coo

D.R Baker

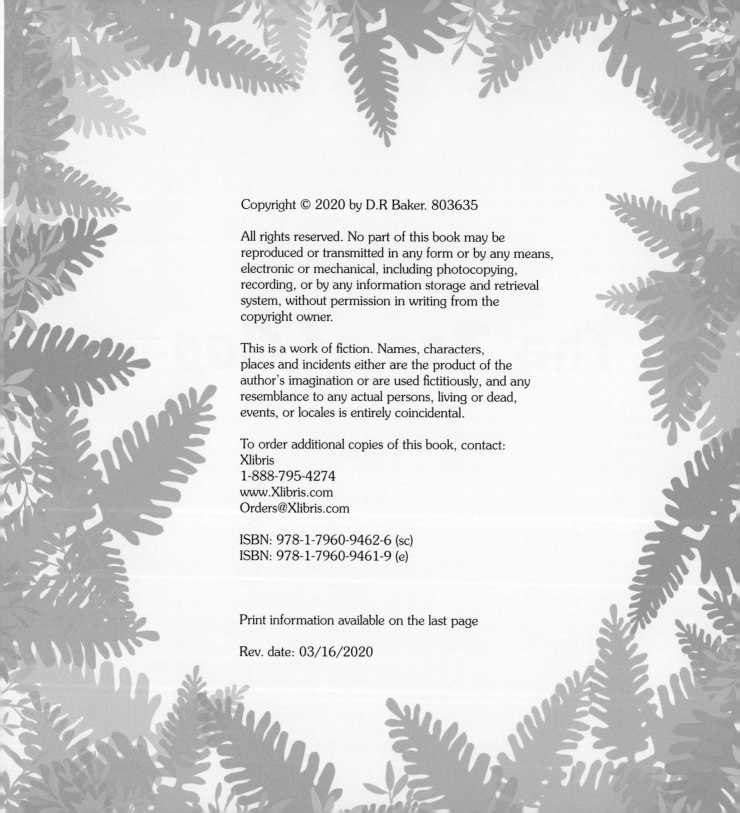

To order additional copies of this book, contact:
Xlibris
1-888-795-4274
www.Xlibris.com
Orders@Xlibris.com

ISBN: 978-1-7960-9462-6 (sc)
ISBN: 978-1-7960-9461-9 (e)

Print information available on the last page

Rev. date: 03/16/2020

Once heard of an old man, named Coo.
He lived in the most wonderful zoo.
Days, months, and years went by, with fun and laughs,but not one cry.
For Coo was not new, his Zoo was his home.
and He did not rule this zoo alone.

This sweet old man was surrounded by friends.
He knew them by ear and he knew them by hand, but Coo knew them not-
by any other sense.
"I need no help!", he loved to boast
yet every morning, they buttered his toast.

His long long life was spent in the night, his friends loved him still,
they made his day bright.
For Coo was blind! And his Zoo was his life,
his friends were so kind, they were nothing but blithe.

Every morning he had breakfast, with family so dear
He knew not what they saw, yet felt it so near.
Coo paid for everything, all the homes for his crew,
all the food and all the tools
His friends ran his zoo, he felt it only right that he do.

But Coo wasn't still, he gave in his own way
For when the zoo closed its gates, Coo began to play!
He strapped a drum to his chest, and a horn in its place,
and coo did this as soon-
as night came from day.

The joy his friends had given, was a debt he tried to repay.
so loud- his drum pounding, and his horn just as strong.
And through the ground- coo felt the sounding
of his friends, dancing along.
There were big thumps, and tiny rumps
and some friends didn't seem
to bump the ground at all!

One afternoon, Coo left the zoo he loved with a bind, for he was wrightly tired
of being blind.
So he left his gates, he left his home, for brightly nightly-knightly roam.
He wanted to see! Coo wanted to know,
"What kind of zoo had made this love grow?"

Villagers that visit the zoo have spoken, of a mountain named Marsalis.
Towering peaks home to creatures of great malice,
but only to those whose heart be ill-balanced.
For when a kind heart draws nearer-
the creatures give solace.
They guide toward tinctures- and miraculous promise.

For the mount is a mirror, and like seeks like.
So on to the tallest mountain, did Coo hike.
"Tall and tough", his friends described, and yet he climbed
All fears aside.

People on the trail helped Coo along his run,
They told him, *"when the end has begun-*
- you'll be brother to the Sun".

As he stood on that peak so high, Coo felt as though he could lay with the sky!
He knew it here, very near, he would see the friends he held so dear.
Coo felt the warmth reach toward his face, he knew it then
He was in the right place.

"There's a Sun within the one,
that is known to you and I"
"Ask It your wish- what your heart may design",
A market man said, with a voice that could shine.
"But ask it pure, where no fear may reside-"
"-for our Sun can hear you, and our Sun has a mind."

So Coo did just that, he asked with his heart.
And once he did- he heard a call from afar!
Wings of a bird grander than most- it blocked the Sun's warmth as it flew close.
Coo was without fear, so he reached toward the sky.
He heard a soft voice, say,
"Your warmth, was once mine."

Then, without speaking-
Coo opened his eyes.

Down the mountain did Coo race, foot after foot, at a frightening pace!
Leap after bound, he began his chase, and not a second did he waste.
Coo saw his Zoo, he could almost reach it!
His life-long beauty, he could finally see it.

But he couldn't believe it, he couldn't help but stare!
"This can't be what I had felt?"
Then Coo rubbed his eyes, and saw a bear-
In a utility belt.

"Oh hey!" Benny said, *"I'll have to tell everyone its Coo!-*
The gate will be done soon, so no one goes in but you."
Bewildered at what his eyes would unfold, Coo trusted the bear,
For his voice was gentle-yet bold.

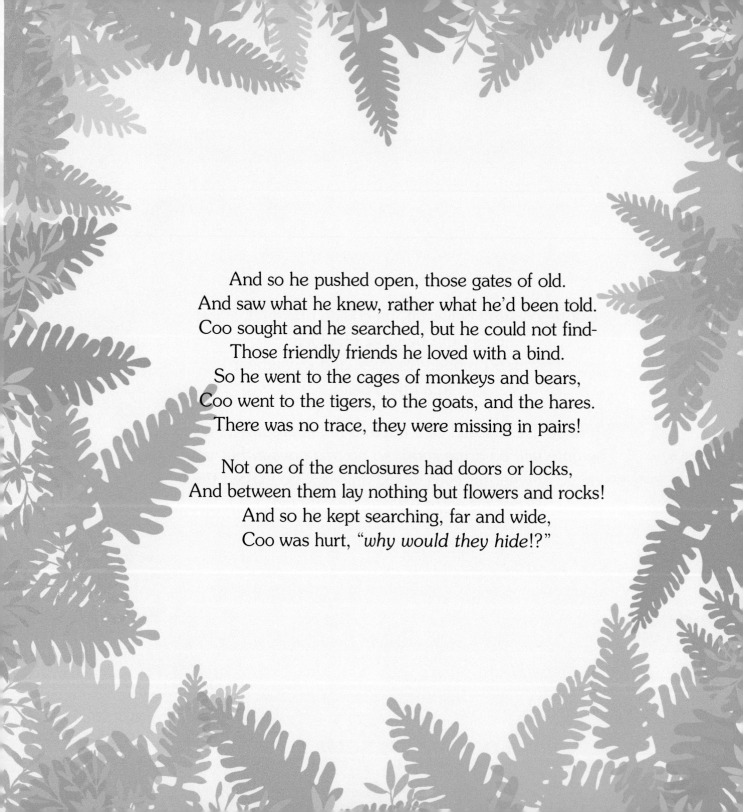

And so he pushed open, those gates of old.
And saw what he knew, rather what he'd been told.
Coo sought and he searched, but he could not find-
Those friendly friends he loved with a bind.
So he went to the cages of monkeys and bears,
Coo went to the tigers, to the goats, and the hares.
There was no trace, they were missing in pairs!

Not one of the enclosures had doors or locks,
And between them lay nothing but flowers and rocks!
And so he kept searching, far and wide,
Coo was hurt, *"why would they hide*!?"

He went to the mess hall, with his head down low, he swung the door open
And little did he know-that his zoo was a wreck, an absolute mess!
In the mess hall, Coo found, a Zoo in distress.
Food everywhere! And no one could guess,
Coo found birds flying clockwise, tigers roaring to impress,
Chameleons is disguise, and two bears wearing vests!
All led by a little monkey in a dress.

"I can't control these animals, my friends had always helped!"
Coo left so that he might see, but now he could tell-
That when Coo left, his friends left as well.
Discouraged and disheartened, he let the wreck be.
Coo turned to the doors and he started to leave.
And as he pushed on, he heard a great plea.
"Coo don't go! Our fun will cease,
we knew you'd return so we made a great feast!
You have a lot left to learn Coo, now that you can see."

Coo Turned around quickly, to meet his old new friends.
He saw no mess, but rather, what sight seems to bend.
A table set neat, and food no meal could beat!
His family sat at the table, where once he thought a stable ought to be.
But a family takes care of each other, and Coo's had saved him a seat.
He joined his friends once again, this Zoo of Coo was now complete.

So now you go, with the company you keep,
Because what you know, isn't always about what you see.

The Zoo of Coo
By: Daniel Baker

~for the love in my life~

Photographed by: Kevin Rose

Born in Plano Illinois.This is Daniel's first book at 23, he wanted to publish the story first for what it's Taught him. It's taught him that life can be simple, and that you don't need to understand everything, just yourself. This table is for readers of all ages, all backgrounds, and class. Ones hope is that you can gain something from this tail, no matter where you are on your journey. "Love is the reason for will of word upon clay"

Printed in the United States
By Bookmasters